Chesapeake and Ohio Early Diesels

by Thomas W. Dixon, Jr.

Designed and Edited by John Krause and Ed Crist

FURTHER READING

For further reading I suggest that readers join the C&O Historical Society, P.O. Box 146, Alderson, West Virginia 24910, and start getting their monthly magazine on the C&O, which often treats of early and modern diesels. The Society has also produced a book, *C&O Diesel Review*, which gives a complete history and roster data on C&O diesels from 1939 to 1982. *C&O Power*, by Staufer Publications, also gives a very good final chapter treatment of the C&O first-generation diesel fleet. First printed in 1965, this book is still in print at this writing.
Thomas W. Dixon, Jr. Alderson, West Virginia August, 1987

FRONT COVER: Ex-Pere Marquette E7 No. 4522 with a two-car Train 26 is seen here at Thompsonville, Michigan in August of 1965. By this time, even though the old PM District lines in Michigan still had several trains in operation, many were of shortened consists like this. As the sixties ended, the old PM units were transferred to the B&O to work out their lives. B&O E7's and -8's and C&O E8's worked what was left of Michigan passenger service until the advent of Amtrak.
C&O Historical Society Collection

Printed in the United States of America.

ISBN 944119-04-2

ANDOVER JUNCTION PUBLICATIONS

BOX 1160, ANDOVER, N.J. 07821

Four Geeps bring a westbound manifest into Russell, Kentucky in 1959. The three-track main accommodated the heaviest traffic on the whole system between Russell and Catlettsburg, a few miles to the east. In 1959, much of American railroading was drifting inexorably into a dreary decade of mergers and abandonments. But the C&O's first-generation fleet continued to haul mountains of coal and miles of freight. The C&O's traditional prosperity and stability would carry it through the turbulent years ahead largely unscathed.
C&O Railway, C&O Historical Society Collection

INTRODUCTION

In the public mind (or at least those who still follow our railroads) and certainly to the railfan community, the name *Chesapeake & Ohio* conjures images of superbly powerful steam locomotives hauling seemingly endless coal trains through the rugged terrain of the Appalachin region. Or perhaps it's the image of the solid, standard *George Washington* from the great days of heavyweight cars and tavern diners of the 1930's and 1940's that is most often called to mind. Whichever of these images the C&O evokes, one does not often think of it as having particularly interesting or innovative diesel locomotives. Neither does one think of the C&O's role in the dieselization of American railroading that occurred forty years ago.

Because the C&O came late to dieselization, its locomotives tended to be proven, off-the-shelf models, mostly built by the Electro-Motive Division of General Motors (EMD). It missed entirely the somewhat romantic period of innovation in diesels that one associates with the Burlington, Santa Fe, or Union Pacific. Its mechanical department, by and large, opted for the products of a single proven builder, with only a small number of locomotives coming from other makers; these were primarily for switching or other special purposes. Only with the coming of the "second generation" of standard diesels did the C&O make any large purchases when it made repeated orders for the General Electric U- and later B-line of locomotives.

This book focuses on the first decade of diesel operations on the C&O, beginning in 1949 and ending in the early 1960's, when the first of the second-generation diesels began to appear on the railway. This was a decade of great change on the C&O, as steam was quickly supplanted and a whole new set of operational philosophies was established. It was also an era of great prosperity for the C&O as its high-quality metallurgical coal found new markets in the post-World War II industrial boom in the United States and in the revitalized industrial capacity of Europe and Japan. Both domestically-consumed and exported coal experienced unprecedented increases in production, though the use of coal for steam generation, home heat, and business suffered a decline because of the competition of oil.

The C&O did not rely heavily on passenger business as did many of the northeastern and midwestern lines. Neither did it depend on less-than-carload freight for any large part of its revenues. So when the bottom fell out of the passenger business and trucks took the lcl market, the C&O still had its great coal-based income. That allowed it not only to weather the economic storm caused by this shift in transportation patterns, but gave it enough surplus money to begin a merger process that eventually led to today's CSX conglomerate.

Before we look at this period of change in the prosperous 1950's, we should give a brief synopsis of C&O history for the general reader.

The C&O's earliest predecessor was the Louisa Railroad, which was incorporated in 1836 to build a line to carry the farm products of Louisa County, to the northwest of Richmond, to market. By 1850, the Louisa had expanded beyond its initial territory and was building towards a great westward expansion. In keeping with these expanded ambitions it changed its name to the Virginia Central. By 1860 it stretched from Richmond to the foot of the Alleghanies, aiming to replace the projected James River & Kanawha Canal in fulfilling the old Virginia dream of the "Great Connection" between the navigation on the James River and that on the "Western Waters" of the Ohio and Mississippi River systems.

However, the Civil War intervened to stop work. In 1868 railroad magnate Collis P. Huntington took control of the company and reorganized it as the C&O, beginning anew the westward expansion. In 1873 the line was completed to the Ohio River at a new city named Huntington in honor of the great man. There the line stayed until 1888 when it was extended down the Kentucky side of the Ohio River to Cincinnati. The decade of the 1890's saw great expansion of branch lines to tap the rich coal and lumber lands of West Virginia and eastern Kentucky as the C&O came under the control of the J.P. Morgan and the Vanderbilt interests. The first decade of the twentieth century saw the C&O pass under the Pennsylvania Railroad's control, further expanding branches and increasing business. By 1911 the C&O had a line to Chicago and had bought control of the Hocking Valley Railway, linking Columbus and southeastern Ohio with Toledo and Great Lakes commerce. This gave the C&O access to the Lakes over friendly lines and the Hocking Valley. From Toledo coal was shipped to the burgeoning industrial Midwest. In 1917 the C&O tired of relying on other lines to get its coal to the Lakes and began construction of a new main line from near Russell, Kentucky to Columbus. This was finally completed in 1926. The Hocking Valley was formally absorbed by the C&O in 1930.

By 1930 the greatest expansion era was over for the C&O. All its coal branches were complete and producing prodigious amounts. Its main lines were among the most solidly built, best engineered, and best maintained in America and its treasury was full. Because of this and the continued strong market for coal, the C&O not only survived the Great Depression unscathed by financial embarrassment, but actually improved its physical plant and took advantage of cheap labor, available materials, and slack traffic to upgrade main lines, enlarge or bore new tunnels, improve grades, and replace bridges. This work positioned it well for the great effort of World War II.

After a superlative performance during the War, the C&O was in a very good position to handle the postwar economic boom.

The C&O's motive power policy up to 1910 had followed standard railroad practices. But beginning in that year the C&O became an innovator in steam locomotive technology, opting for heavier and more powerful engines to pull its heavy coal trains over the Virginias' Alleghany Mountain and across the flatlands of Ohio. By 1930 it was firmly in the "Super Power" camp of Lima Locomotive Works. From then until the arrival of diesels, the C&O was looked up to as one of the innovators in the steam arena. Beginning in the 1930's the diesel builders brought the diesel-electric locomotive from experimental to production status. The War served to accelerate this process, which became very rapid in the immediate postwar years. But of all the railroads embracing the new technology, the C&O was the one that steadfastly refused to buy diesels for any purpose. The philosophy of its management was that since coal was the C&O's principal commodity, it should do everything possible to promote it. This included using coal as the fuel for the railroad.

Although C&O management was solidly anti-oil and anti-diesel, they nontheless realized that the reciprocating steam locomotive as it had been known over the last century was doomed as the principal motive power for American railroads. The C&O began an aggressive campaign to develop alternatives to reciprocating steam that would still use coal. One project was the Steam-Turbine-Electric locomotive and another was a coal-gas-turbine engine. The Steam-Turbine-Electric was actually built by the C&O, American Locomotive Company, and General Electric. This giant locomotive was intended to power a flashy, new high-technology passenger train called *The Chessie*. The train was also tied to the C&O's campaign to save passenger service through updated equipment, fast schedules, and outstanding service. Both the turbine and *The Chessie* were part of C&O Chairman Robert Young's crusade to bring railroading up to date and eliminate the railroad's reliance on 19th-century technology and the equally-antiquated thinking of railroad managements. He made a great stir in the decade after World War II, using the rock-solid C&O as his platform. Young ultimately used C&O money to buy him the New York Central's chairmanship. Once he had that job, he was forced to quit his C&O position and the C&O reverted to a less strident posture. But it nevertheless remained firmly in the camp of progressive railroads with an innovative management, a research department that served as a "think tank" for technological innovations, and a solid financial basis for the future.

The Steam-Turbine-Electric failed in service and were retired within a year of their arrival. The C&O experienced a great financial crisis in 1949 as a result of the convergence of several circumstances. First, it had largely rebuilt the Mountain Subdivision over the Blue Ridge and Shenandoah ranges between Charlottesville and Clifton

Forge, Virginia. This line hadn't been upgraded since its construction in the 1850's. In addition, major realignments, new tunnels, grade reductions, bridge reconstructions, and other improvements were made in the 1944-1949 period that required the outlay of tremendous sums. Second, during this time the passenger business had suddenly become a losing proposition. Finally, a major coal mine strike in 1949 resulted in the mines working only 170 days that year, thus drastically restricting C&O's cash flow by throttling its principal commodity. During these years C&O had also invested heavily in new rolling stock and motive power. All this left the railway financially embarrassed for the first time in the present century, forcing some decisions that Young really didn't want to make. The financial analysts that Young had hired to steer the C&O into the gleaming future he envisioned finally found an audience for their conclusion that dieselization made sense.

So it was that in 1949 C&O management caved in on the diesel question and the first batch of switchers was purchased for the old C&O lines. C&O President Walter Touhy announced in a news release in May, 1949, "It appears to us that there are very substantial savings in the use of diesels for switching purposes only." In that year, 142 diesels were ordered for both the old C&O lines (now called the Chesapeake District) and the former Pere Marquette lines (now called the PM District or Northern Region). All of these were switchers except for a few road diesels for the PM lines.

The old Pere Marquette lines in Michigan and Canada had already been C&O's proving ground for diesels. The PM had been formed in 1899 out of a maze of smaller Michigan roads that had crystallized into three major systems by then. The PM, growing prosperous with the developing automotive industry in Michigan, came under C&O influence in the 1920's as part of the great railroad empire assembled by O.P. and M.J. Van Sweringen of Cleveland. The brothers put together a system based first on the Nickel Plate and later the C&O. The PM remained independent, but wholly owned by the C&O, until 1947, when it was merged into the main system. In 1939 the PM had bought its first diesel, followed by another in 1942 and several more in the 1942-1945 period. Logically, they were products of General Motor's Electro-Motive Division since GM was one of the railroad's biggest shippers. These SW1's and NW2's were used to dieselize several important switching areas and were quite well received.

In 1946 the Pere Marquette inaugurated the country's first postwar streamliners, the *Pere Marquettes*. These were seven-car lightweight coach trains running between Detroit and Grand Rapids on expedited schedules and were to prove Young's theory that good passenger trains could beat automobile, bus, and airline competition. They were powered by two EMD E7-model passenger diesels. Six more E7's came to the PM in 1947, and a final two units in 1948 (after the C&O merger) dieselized all of the Pere Marquette's passenger service. In 1948, also, more switchers just about eliminated steam switching from the railway. Thus in 1949 the C&O planners had several years of both switching and road diesel performance statistics to look at. Yet the C&O's philosophy was still firmly committed to coal-burning locomotives as the only proper motive power for coal-hauling trains. Even while the PM lines were being given diesels, C&O management ordered 105 new steam locomotives for the old C&O lines! It was certainly a house divided in its localities and basic philosophies. This last great lot of steam consisted of 15 of the C&O's giant 2-6-6-6 simple articulated "Allegheny" types, 40 of its workhorse 2-8-4's (called "Kanawha" types on the C&O) for freight work, five of the 4-8-4's and five of the 4-6-4's for passengers, 30 of the 0-8-0's for the yards, and ten plodding 2-6-6-2 compounds for coal mine shifter runs. The 0-8-0's were hardly a year old when the decision to dieselize yard work was made, and many were sold to the all-steam Virginian and Norfolk & Western.

The 1949 diesel order for the C&O lines saw the arrival of 20 EMD NW2's and 58 S-2 switchers from Alco. There were also three sets of EMD TR3 hump engines, which were essentially an NW2 semi-permanently joined to two cabless boosters, all for yard work. Then, in 1950, the idea of using diesels in road freight service finally gained a foothold and the Chicago Division was completely dieselized with the purchase of 16 three-unit A-B-A EMD F7 road freight haulers. This was a logical line on which to test the road diesels since it was a fairly flat line across Indiana, far removed from the pressures of coal operator customers. It was a line haul operation with few switching districts and no branches. It had bridge and clearance restrictions that precluded the use of modern steam power; standard steam power on the line had been 2-8-2 Mikados built in 1923-24. It also was not very visible, since the last passenger trains — mere locals — had been removed in 1949.

With the success of the F7's on the Chicago Division well established, the C&O's motive power men ordered 27 more sets of A-B-A units in late 1951 for delivery in the spring of 1952. These units were used system-wide and completely dieselized road freight work on the Ohio lines. A final four sets in late 1952 rounded out the 141 F7's that the C&O owned.

To supplement the passenger fleet and make locomotives available to handle troop trains and specials as well as some secondary runs, the C&O bought seven sets of A-B-A FP7's in early 1952 and an additional two sets in 1953 for a total of 24 of these units. They were used on passenger runs when needed, and when not were most often seen on manifest freight where their high gear ratio could be put to best advantage. With the arrival of these units, the C&O fleet of cabs was complete at 165. But it was the end of the cab unit era in American railroading and the road switcher was ascendant.

From May of 1952 to April of 1954, the Chesapeake District received 101 GP7's that had proved so successful in completely killing steam on the Pere Marquette District. Twenty-six Alco RSD-5 road units arrived in May and June of 1952 for use on coal drags between Russell and Toledo and later in hump yard service. The GP9 model from EMD was purchased beginning in December of 1954 and by August of 1957 numbered 363 units on the Chesapeake District. Finally 22 Alco RSD-12 and RSD-7 heavy road freight engines arrived in 1956 and were concentrated in the Logan, West Virginia coalfields, replacing the 2-6-6-2 compound Mallets on mine runs and on the mainline from Logan to Russell.

Steam's last stand came in 1955-56 when an upturn in export coal business as well as a boom in domestic production (thus spurring the metallurgical coal business and merchandise and automobile traffic) caught the C&O short of power. So much steam had been retired during the Korean War that diesel orders couldn't catch up fast enough. Thus the C&O reactivated the newest of its steamers, which were still stored and could be brought back to life with the least work. So in 1955 and 1956 steam locomotives that had been retired for as much as two to three years were back on the road thumbing their noses at the diesels. But not for long. The reactivated steamers were used mainly on the Hinton Division between Hinton and Handley, West Virginia and in the Logan coal district where the 2-6-6-2 Mallets had never given up. The final chapter of steam closed with the arrival of the last orders of GP9's and RSD-12's and -7's in 1956. The last steamer to run was an old H-6 2-6-6-2 out of Peach Creek Yard in Logan in October of 1956. After that the only steam operations on the C&O were for excursions.

Meanwhile back on the PM District the C&O had purchased 14 of EMD's BL2 model locomotives. These strange and rare engines were a transition model between EMD's road freight units and the road switcher and were built only in limited numbers. The 14 units that C&O bought in 1948 and 1949 constituted 24% of the entire fleet that EMD built. They were all lettered C&O but had a distinctive PM paint scheme settled on before the merger. In 1950, 20 of EMD's GP7-model road switchers arrived on the PM District, followed the next year by 98 more, thus eliminating steam from the Michigan and Canada lines by mid-1951.

On the Chesapeake District between 1950 and 1952, 42 Baldwin heavy road switchers of the AS-616 model were installed for transfer, hump, and heavy switching service. They were used mainly at Columbus, Russell, Kentucky (where the C&O had the largest yard owned by a single road), and Huntington, West Virginia, and on the steep grade from Cincinnati west to Cheviot, Ohio on the Chicago Division.

Probably the most visible and symbolic move was made in May of 1951 when 27 EMD E8 passenger units arrived and dieselized most of the C&O's passenger service almost overnight, banishing the world's heaviest Hudsons and the famed "Greenbrier" 4-8-4 types to freight service and sending Pacifics and smaller passenger steamers to the scrapper. In May of 1953, four additional E8's rounded out the C&O fleet of this model.

The original publicity releases on the purchase of diesels said that the C&O was buying these units because analysis showed that they could pay for themselves in overall economies in four to five years. By that time the C&O expected the gas or coal turbine locomotive to be ready for production. The argument went that when this occurred, the diesels would be sold and the C&O would revert to coal as a fuel, using the new technology that was then being actively pursued by a consortium of railroads and one of the steam locomotive builders. Of course time would prove that the economies of the diesels made them so popular that the difficult research to perfect a coal-powered engine languished and eventually collapsed. By the early 1950's it was obvious that the fate of the reciprocating steam locomotive on the C&O was sealed. The cheap price of fuel oil, the economies gained by less shop time and easier roadbed maintenance offset their initial high per-unit cost. In particular, the downward thrust of the reciprocating parts of a steam locomotive—known as "dynamic augment"—had made roadway maintenance exacting and expensive, but the smooth torque of the diesels eliminated the need for constant roadbed work. All of these savings became more and more evident in the 1950-54 period as steam was progressively edged out, even though C&O management still maintained that they intended to use steam for the foreseeable future where it proved more economical than diesels.

It's interesting to note that the C&O stuck with one builder for most of its initial diesel orders, but since General Motors was so important a customer it's not surprising either. Alco supplied some C&O engines, but soon faded from the scene. The C&O's favorite builder of modern steam, Lima, never supplied a single diesel to the C&O's fleet.

There were no orders for engines of any type between 1957 and 1962. The Geeps and F's held sway on the mainlines and branches alike, with the F's, of course, usually appearing on manifest freight trains and run-throughs while the Geeps showed up in almost any duty as befitted their general-purpose name. The heavy coal trains over Alleghany Mountain from Hinton to Clifton Forge, that had required a 2-6-6-6 Allegheny type in front and back, now rolled over the 0.57-percent, 14-mile grade with four or five Geeps up front. At first the railway used two or three in front with two helping, the helpers cutting off at Alleghany, Virginia and returning to Hinton. But soon it was decided to use all the power up front. Pushers on this grade weren't revived until the 1980's. The E8's handled passengers easily as trains were eliminated over the years and the fleet remained largely intact until they began to be transferred to the B&O after the C&O/B&O affiliation in 1963. The B&O had more passenger service than the C&O and its locomotives were older and wearing out.

The first of what has become known as the "second generation" of diesels were ordered in 1962 and delivered in 1963, just a little over a decade after the arrival of the first road engines and only seven years after the disappearance of steam. The first class of diesels to leave the C&O was the EMD BL2's. These 14 engines were traded in to EMD in the summer of 1962 for GP30's to be delivered that fall.

In the 1962-through-1965 period the C&O got 48 GP30's, 19 SD18's, 38 U-25B's, 36 GP35's, and 12 SD35's. All these models were from favorite EMD except the U-25B's, which were from General Electric. From that time forward the C&O began splitting its orders between EMD and GE as the second-generation fleet expanded. The SD18's and the U-25B's were first used on the old mainline across Alleghany Mountain, but eventually were reassigned, the SD18's to switching and hump yard duties at Russell and Handley, and the U-25B's to the Michigan lines. In the 1960's and 1970's, the second-generation fleet expanded and replaced the first-generation diesels much in the way the latter had replaced steam, as massive orders of GP38, GP39, GP40, GP40-2, SD40, U-23B, U-30C, and GE's B-series units arrived. Alco's only entry in the second-generation competition was a set of C-630's bought in 1967 and sold in 1974. The first-generation units soon began to be transferred to the B&O after that road was taken over by the C&O, since it was in need of power. The entire fleet of C&O F-units went to the B&O in 1963 and 1964, where they fit right in with the huge fleet of F's that the B&O had. Having dieselized much earlier than the C&O, the B&O had been in on the heyday of the cab unit that the C&O missed. The Alco and Baldwin switchers and road engines also found their way to the B&O in the mid-1960's and worked there for about a decade before scrapping. The Geep fleet was eventually sold, scrapped, or downgraded to yard work to replace switchers that were largely eliminated in the 1970's and early 1980's. By the early 1980's it was hard to find a Geep on a mainline train.

The E7's were transferred to the B&O in the mid-1960's and many of the E8's went there in the late 1960's as well, before scrapping. The last E-units were off the C&O a year or two after Amtrak's takeover of passenger service in 1971, since the new company didn't buy any C&O units. Of the first generation, few survive. The C&O Museum now holds a Pere Marquette SW1 that dates from 1942, and it's still running, carrying museum visitors on a short ride around Baltimore. In the 1970's, C&O, B&O, and Western Maryland power under Chessie System was totally consolidated and intermixed. Beginning in about 1985, Chessie and Seaboard System power began to be totally integrated and in 1986 a new CSX paint scheme was devised, thus beginning the cycle again of erasing the last vestiges of the old order and installing a new era.

C&O Railway, C&O Historical Society Collection

PAINT SCHEMES

Of course, the earliest units on the C&O lines were on the Pere Marquette. The 1939-1942 SW1's were painted black with steam-engine lettering on their hoods. Later PM switchers had blue paint with yellow stripes back from the nose, trimmed in red pinstripes. The BL2's had a distinctive scheme using blue and gray with stripes and a script road name. The PM E7's were blue, silver and yellow to match the paint scheme of the new lightweight passenger cars. The Geeps all came after the C&O merger and were solid blue with yellow stripes and lettering in the style of that used on steam locomotive tenders as well as the famous "C&O For Progress" herald. Switchers were blue with yellow decoration and lettering again in the Railroad Roman style of the steam era.

J&D Studios Collection

J&D Studios Collection

On the C&O, the blue basic scheme with yellow stripes and lettering became standard on all units except the F's and E's. The first F's arrived with a blue body and a thick yellow stripe at the bottom. The nose was covered with a yellow "bow wave" that formed a "V" right under the headlight. The road name appeared on the sides in C&O script, made famous by its appearance on the letterboards on the new lightweight passenger cars of 1950. The later F7 orders stuck to this scheme, but lowered the height of the bow wave. When major shopping was done in the mid-1950's, some of the F's were repainted to a simpler scheme that eliminated the bow wave and substituted a plain "Futura Demibold" lettering for the road name. Finally, when they were in the process of being transferred to the B&O, they were given an even simpler scheme of solid blue with only a large C&O on the side. Some were relettered B&O, while some kept their C&O designations until their end. A few remained in the old wave paint scheme until scrapping in the late 1960's and early 1970's.

The E7's went through a similar metamorphosis. Starting out with the PM designs, they were later all converted to the C&O's three-color scheme used on the E8's and then to the solid blue with the big lettering described for the F's while in service on the B&O. Likewise some of them were lettered B&O as well and some went to scrap in the C&O three-color paint. The C&O E8's arrived in two schemes. The first 10 received were exactly like the F's with the yellow bow wave, but the second 17 were painted in a three-color scheme of basic blue, with a wide band of silver/gray on the bottom, and a narrow band of yellow at the top. These colors harmonized and blended in with the schemes on the passenger cars they pulled. The road name appeared in script on the flanks, and the famous "For progress" emblem was on the nose. Starting in 1967, some were repainted to a simplified scheme with no yellow, a simple gray band on the bottom and a big C&O on the side. Some also got the solid blue paint treatment and were relettered B&O. A few went to scrap in the three-color sheme. The first ten were repainted to the three-color scheme within two years of delivery, making it by far the rarest of the liveries of this class.

The ubiquitous GP7's and 9's began with a simple blue body, yellow accent stripes starting at a "V" on the ends and drawn horizontal on the sides. Early units had a "C&O For Progress" herald in a yellow disk. Later units had the herald in yellow against a solid blue background. The old steam Railroad Roman lettering adorned the sides, later to be replaced by the sans serif "Futura Demibold" style. Like the other units, they eventually got the solid blue with B&O/C&O scheme. Some went to WM or B&O lettering while others retained one of the other schemes until their end.

Second-generation schemes were generally simpler. The first units had a "Futura Demibold" road name and yellow noses for visibility. Later this changed to a solid blue and a big C&O on the sides, and the "For progress" herald on a blue nose. In 1972, the Chessie System paint scheme of all-yellow, blue lettering, and vermillion accent striping came into existence and by the CSX merger most C&O and B&O units were wearing this paint.

J&D Studios Collection

The accompanying map shows the C&O system about as it appeared in 1960. In the photographic portion of this book we will travel over the system beginning at Washington, D.C. and Newport News, Virginia and end on the Canadian Division.

The C&O operates on trackage rights over the Southern Railway from Washington to Orange, Virginia, where it picks up its own Washington Subdivision line to Charlottesville. The Peninsula Subdivision begins at the docks at Newport News and comes to Richmond. Here the Piedmont Subdivision, which is the original Louisa Railroad line, goes northwest to Charlottesville, while the James River line follows the river to its origin at Clifton Forge. From Charlottesville, the Mountain Subdivision crosses the Blue Ridge and Shenandoah ranges and joins with the James River line at Clifton Forge.

West of Clifton Forge the Alleghany Subdivision crosses its namesake mountain and terminates at Hinton, West Virginia, at the beginning of the New River gorge. The New River Subdivision then follows that river to Handley, West Virginia, where it becomes the Kanawha Subdivision, following that river to St. Albans and then across country to Huntington and across the Big Sandy River at its confluence with the Ohio River into Russell, Kentucky. Russell, with its massive yard and junction of so many lines, was a subdivision to itself only seven miles long. From Ashland, near Russell, the Lexington-Louisville Subdivision went west to its namesake cities, half on C&O track and half over L&N trackage rights. West of Russell the Northern Subdivision branches off the Cincinnati Division mainline and goes north to Columbus, where it joins the old Hocking Valley lines for the trip to Toledo. The Hocking Valley lines southeast of Columbus were once heavy coal producers but were of little importance in modern times.

West from Russell the mainline hugs the Kentucky bank of the Ohio River until it arrives at Covington, opposite Cincinnati. It then vaults across the great river and into the Queen City. From Cincinnati the Chicago Division makes a nearly straight diagonal line across Indiana to Chicago.

The old/Pere Marquette lines honeycomb Michigan and extend into Ontario, with trackage rights on the New York Central mainline through to Buffalo. Important mainlines in Michigan are Toledo-Detroit-Flint-Saginaw, Ludington-Saginaw, Detroit-Grand Rapids-Chicago, and Detroit-St. Thomas-Buffalo.

Branch lines play an important part in the C&O picture, with the New River and Kanawha Subdivisions hosting junction points for many coal districts, each boasting scores of subordinate branches. Eastern Kentucky has the Big Sandy line entering the main near Ashland. In the east, the Hot Springs line was important only for passengers, and the Greenbrier branch declined in importance as lumbering in the area played out in the 1940's and 1950's.

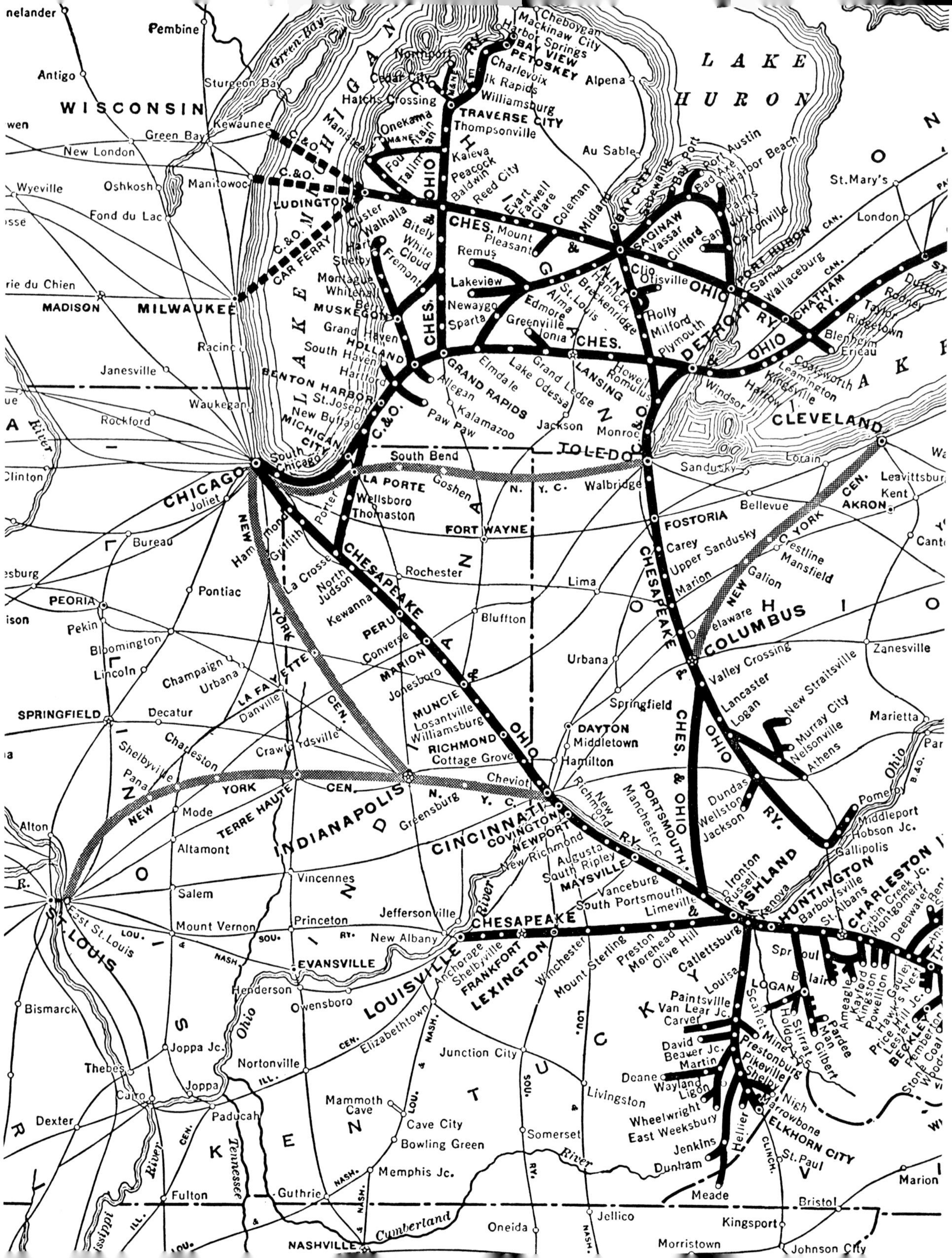

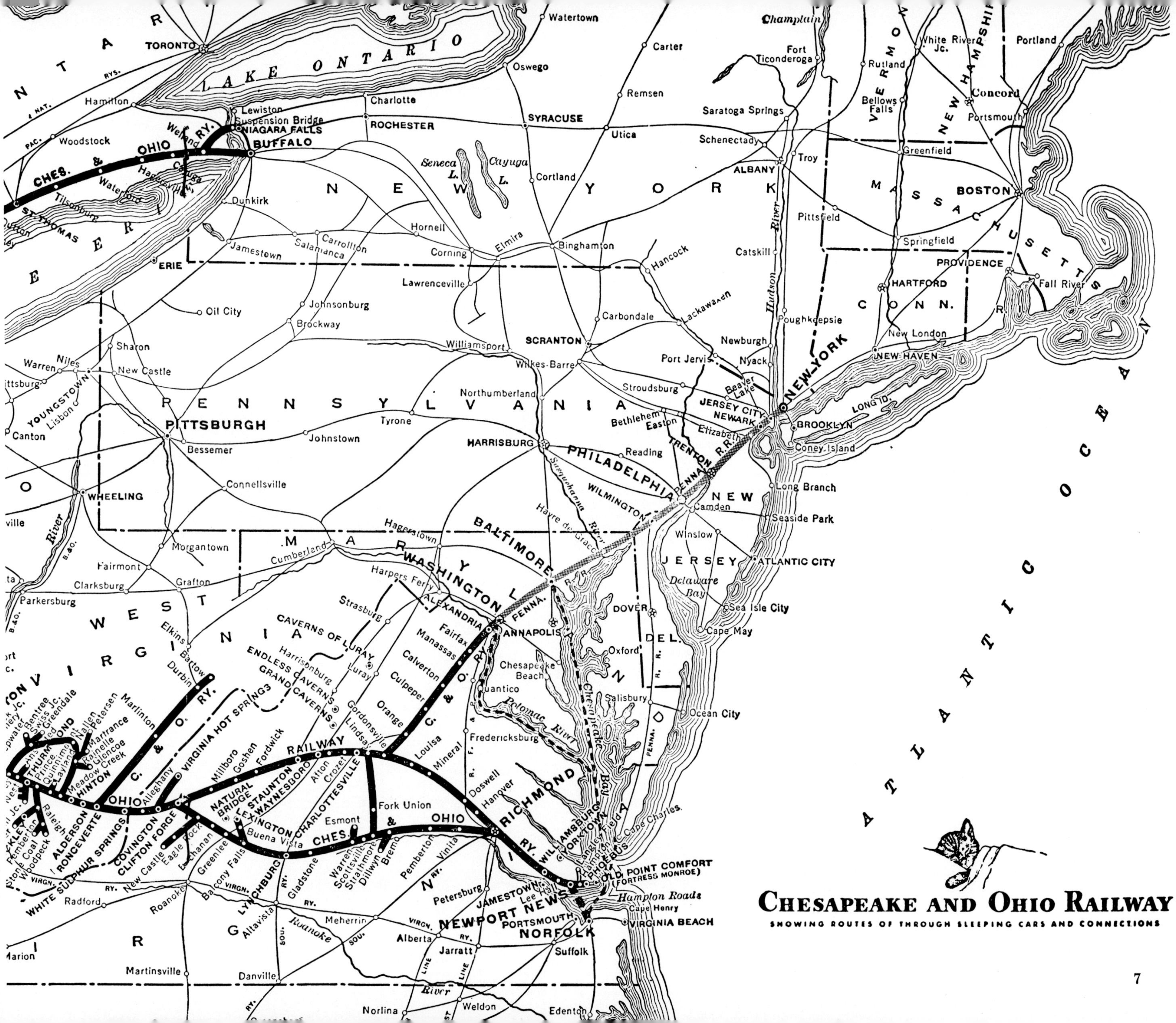

Chesapeake and Ohio Railway

SHOWING ROUTES OF THROUGH SLEEPING CARS AND CONNECTIONS

For passengers, the C&O began at Washington Union Station, or if you count through cars, at Pennsylvania Station in New York City. In the late 1880's trackage rights agreements with the Virginia Midland (now Southern Railway) allowed the C&O into the nation's capitol and agreements with the Pennsylvania Railroad allowed through cars and sometimes entire through trains there from New York. These arrangements continued until Amtrak's takeover. Here C&O E8 No. 4005 and a mate have the *George Washington*, Train 1, at Washington taking on mail, express, baggage, and passengers for the trek through the Virginias and Kentucky to Cincinnati. This particular day, April 24, 1957, the train is celebrating its 25th anniversary and that was the occasion for the company photographer to be on hand to record this image.
C&O Railway, C&O Historical Society Collection

Washington was an important point of termination for both the C&O and the B&O, and was a logical spot for the public relations department to photograph motive power of the two roads together in December of 1961, the pictures to be used in news releases about the proposed "affiliation" of the two lines. Of course, this affiliation was effected and grew to total merger. Here C&O E8 No. 4001 and B&O E7 No. 1424 sit on the radial tracks of Washington's Ivy City engine terminal in the winter of 1961, when passenger trains were still important to America.
C&O Railway, C&O Historical Society Collection

The C&O had two passenger terminals of importance on its eastern ends, the first at Washington and the second at the great deepwater harbor of Hampton Roads, at Newport News. Here ferries carried passengers to and from Norfolk and Portsmouth on the south side of the harbor to meet the trains that originated on this pier on the Newport News side. Here C&O E8 No. 4015 is shown in April of 1970, in its very last days, wearing the simplified paint scheme that came into vogue in the late 1960's for all C&O power. From here trains connected with other trains coming from Washington at Charlottesville, Virginia, where they were combined to run as a single train to Ashland, Kentucky, where sections were again broken up to go to Cincinnati and Louisville as well as Detroit.
Thomas W. Dixon, Jr.

F7 No. 7035, leading an A-B-A set, is shown here with an empty coal train out of the huge Newport News yards. Coal was the lifeblood of the C&O, and it was carried from West Virginia and Kentucky eastward to Newport News for shipment by sea up the coast and to foreign countries. Westward, it went to the Great Lakes at Toledo. The 7035 is wearing the second F-unit paint scheme, adopted about the time this photo was taken in 1957, which eliminated the "bow wave" yellow paint on its nose and placed a sans serif lettering on its flanks.
C&O Railway, C&O Historical Society Collection

Troop trains were still frequent when this photo was taken in May of 1959 at Ft. Eustis, Virginia. GP9 No. 6086 was one of several equipped with a steam generator. It has brought a train of heavyweight cars to the Army's extensive private railroad at Ft. Eustis, which was and is the transportation center for the Army.
H.L. Buckley, Jr. Collection

This obviously posed public relations photo shows F7 No. 7022 and kin with C&O's manifest freight No. 90, known as ***The Expediter***, as it nears the eastern end of its run from Chicago to Newport news, here on the Peninsula Subdivision just east of Richmond in 1957. The first F's were without the Mars lights in the door and had the "high wave" paint that extended above the marker lights.
C&O Railway, C&O Historical Society Collection

This photo is out of our time period, but is used to illustrate the last paint scheme that the GP7's and other units went through before the arrival of the yellow Chessie System design. This is the solid blue with the large C&O on the sides and the heralds on the hood. The same scheme was used on B&O units as well. This photo was taken at Richmond's Fulton Yard in 1972.
Thomas W. Dixon, Jr.

GP7 No. 6212 and two other units hasten an eastbound manifest over the great James River viaduct at Richmond in February of 1964, carrying reefers, boxcars, and flats with machinery. The viaduct was built around 1901 to connect the C&O's water-level James River line with the Peninsula Subdivision. It was built for several miles along the north side of the James River, actually in the bed of the river part of the way and over city streets in other places. As this photo illustrates, it was almost constantly being repaired and renewed.
C&O Railway, C&O Historical Society Collection

Main Street Station in Richmond, built jointly by the C&O and Seaboard Air Line in 1901-1903, is the C&O's principal contribution to big-station architecture in America. Its French Renaissance headhouse connects with the impressive trainshed, which served the C&O on the left and the SAL on the right. For a time Southern trains serving Richmond visited here as well. In this 1954 view, E8 No. 4027 had a six-car Virginia section underway westbound to its Charlottesville rendezvous. Two lightweight cars space the four heavyweights in its consist.
C&O Railway, C&O Historical Society Collection

E8 No. 4022 brings Train 4, *The Sportsman*, over the crest of the Blue Ridge at Afton, Virginia, in June of 1961. The three locomotives have 12 cars in tow this day as they top the Blue Ridge, one of three mountain barriers the C&O challenges in its trek across the Virginias. Just a few miles to the east the train will be broken up at Charlottesville, with one unit taking five cars to Richmond and Newport News, while two units take the rest, plus some added at Charlottesville, on to Washington.
William E. Warden

Four GP7's and -9's have a westbound freight in tow just west of Afton, Virginia station. To the photographer's back is Blue Ridge Tunnel, the original bore of which was built by the famed civil engineer Claudius Crozet in the mid-1850's. Crozet, an army engineer and a refugee from his native France at the end of the Napoleonic Wars, established much of the engineering curriculum at West Point. He then became involved as Virginia's Chief Engineer in implementing a transportation plan of roads, canals, and railroads. His last achievement was to almost single-handedly establish Virginia Military Institute. Crozet's landmark tunnel was replaced by a new bore in the early 1940's. Stretching out to the east in this 1957 view is the Piedmont section of Virginia.
C&O Railway, C&O Historical Society Collection

The Sportsman, Train No. 4, was easy to photograph in Virginia since it ran from mid-morning to mid-afternoon through the state eastbound. Here the standard consist of three E8's and 16 cars slides east on the Mountain Subdivision at Longdale, just east of Clifton Forge, in September of 1959. Number 4 carried a lot of head-end business and a lot of passengers in those now almost forgotten days not so long ago!
C&O Railway, C&O Historical Society Collection

This October, 1956 view shows a westbound passenger train, probably No. 5, *The Sportsman*, entering the yard limit at Clifton Forge, Virginia, with two E8's for power. An S-2 switcher lurks on the Jackson River bridge to the right with what is probably a local freight off the Craig Valley branch. This is the spot where the Mountain Subdivision on the left and the James River line on the right diverge. The Mountain goes to Richmond via Waynesboro, Staunton, and Charlottesville and over the Shenandoah and Blue Ridge grades. The James River line follows that river through Lynchburg to Richmond, cutting through those mountain ranges rather than going over them. E8 No. 4025 still has its coupler cowl in place and no m.u. plug on its nose. These were added about this time so units could run in other than pairs. The coupler cowls were removed for the same reason.
C&O Railway, C&O Historical Society Collection

Clifton Forge, Virginia, is the C&O's great classification yard and shop facility that lies at the base of the Alleghany range and has served as the resting point, crew change area, and shop facility for trains coming and going on the James River and Mountain Subdivisions to the east and the Alleghany Subdivision to the west. This 1957 photo shows a shining fresh set of Geeps probably getting ready to go west, since the C&O always operated its units short hood forward, unlike neighboring Norfolk & Western that always operated with the long hood ahead.
C&O Railway, C&O Historical Society Collection

This brace of F7's idles near the depot at Clifton Forge between assignments. They show the "low wave" paint scheme of the second F-unit order where the bow wave doesn't go over the marker lights and the nose door has a Mars light in it. The icing platform stands in the background.
C&O Railway, C&O Historical Society Collection

Three Geeps run past the streamlined coal dock built in 1947 to service the ill-fated steam turbines at Clifton Forge. Additional Geeps work in the yard in the distance in July of 1957.
C&O Railway, C&O Historical Society Collection

Here a single E8 powers eastbound mail and express train No. 104, stopped for station work at Covington, Virginia, in 1956. The red Mars light (the upper of two headlights) was used in the early days only for emergencies. In later days it was replaced with a standard white Mars light that was used at all times. The unit hasn't gotten the m.u. receptacle yet nor lost it coupler cowl.
C&O Railway, C&O Historical Society Collection

The Hot Springs branch was built as a passenger line to link the C&O mainline at Covington with the popular Homestead hotel resort at Hot Springs. C&O President M. E. Ingalls loved Hot Springs and in 1891 had the 25-mile branch built to his favorite resort and summer home. In later years the train carried not only the Pullmans from New York and Washington (and many other places on special occasions) but also freight, usually coal for the hotel's steam plant. Here the mixed train switches its caboose, heavyweight combine, and lightweight 11-double-bedroom Pullman at the Hot Springs yard in September of 1955. The unusual device on the roof of GP7 No. 5829 is a steam generator exhaust pipe.
Gene Huddleston C&O Historical Society Collection

These two photos were taken at the same time at Moss Run, Virginia, a few miles west of Covington and east of Alleghany on the very steep westbound Alleghany climb. The first shows a standard consist of five Geeps tugging hard on a westbound train of empties. The second shows brake shoes smoking as a loaded train is restrained on its eastward descent of the grade. By the time these photos were taken — about 1957 — the lashup of five Geeps was standard for coal and manifests between Clifton Forge and Hinton, West Virginia, replacing the massive 2-6-6-6 simple articulateds that had done the job before.
C&O Railway, C&O Historical Society Collection

ABOVE LEFT:
Rolling downgrade at Callaghan, Virginia, an eastbound manifest filled out with coal is powered by a set of FP7's. When not working special passenger movements, these units regularly worked fast freights. In the background is Alleghany Mountain, over which the train has just come. This photo was taken about 1953. Note that the FP are painted just like the E8's, with the three-color scheme for passenger service.
C&O Railway, C&O Historical Society Collection

RIGHT; ABOVE AND BELOW:
These two photos show trains near Jerry's Run fill at the top of Alleghany Mountain. The fill was, for several decades, the largest railroad fill in the world and was completed in 1873 when the C&O was built westward from Clifton Forge across West Virginia. The rugged and isolated mountain scenery is a fine setting for photography. The first photo shows F's in the second paint scheme with a westbound freight struggling hard upgrade. The second shows two FP7's with an all-mail-and-express train handling the Christmas business. Both views date to December of 1957.
Gene Huddleston, C&O Historical Society Collection

The westernmost photograph possible in Virginia is at Alleghany Tunnel. The border with West Virginia runs through the center of the tunnel. This 1952 photo shows the transition of power on the C&O. Nearly hidden on the left is a massive 2-6-6-6 Allegheny type, No. 1601, which has just pushed the coal drag to the top. Emerging from the other bore of the tunnel is a manifest freight in the control of a set of F7's.
B. F. Cutler

A brace of F7's brings manifest freight No. 95 downgrade and westbound out of Alleghany Tunnel on May 30, 1957. The 7074 in the lead is still in the wave paint but the trailing units have been repainted to the simpler scheme. Note the different road name lettering as well. The train is in both Virginia and West Virginia at this point.
Gene Huddleston, C&O Historical Society Collection

The C&O had many center passing sidings, most of which were removed soon after the end of steam. Here a set of Geeps, led by the 5936, brings a coal drag up Alleghany grade at Tuckahoe, West Virginia. Just behind the photographer is Alleghany Tunnel at the top of the grade. Alco S-4 switcher No. 5101 holds the center siding with a ditcher/spreader. The coal train is moving at about only 8 mph on this warm and clear May 30, 1957.
Gene Huddleston, C&O Historical Society Collection

The standard five Geeps brings a coal drag east upgrade past the C&O's showplace depot at White Sulphur Springs, West Virginia. Behind the trees in the background is the C&O-owned resort hotel, The Greenbrier, famous as a "watering place" in Virginia since Colonial times, the haunt of presidents from Martin Van Buren to Dwight Eisenhower. The 11-double-bedroom Pullman *Greenbrier* is in one of the pullman park tracks, which could accommodate a full train and often did. White Sulphur Springs was a very important passenger station, generating tremendous revenues, especially from the eastern cities as people vacationed here or attended conventions. Geep No. 6258 is in the simplified paint scheme without stripes and using the "Futura Demibold" lettering.
C&O Railway, C&O Historical Society Collection

Flying white flags, C&O E7's still carrying the Pere Marquette lettering, one in C&O tri-colors and the second still in original colors, speed an all-heavyweight Pullman special east at Ronceverte, West Virginia, bound for the Greenbrier, probably from Detroit.
C&O Railway, C&O Historical Society Collection

Eastbound Train 4, *The Sportsman*, headed by E8 No. 4003, found a strange little wanderer at the Ronceverte station in December of 1965. Shay No. 7 had been purchased by Cass Scenic from the Meadow River Lumber Company. With a C&O caboose in tow, the Shay had come down the branch from Rainelle to Meadow Creek, West Virginia and then east on the main line to Roncerverte. After laying over at Ronceverte during the night, the Shay is seen here preparing to make the final leg of its journey from Ronceverte up the branch to Cass and a new career.
John P. Killoran, J&D Studios Collection

Four Geeps burst from Fort Spring Tunnel at Fort Spring, West Virginia, in May of 1957 carrying an eastbound coal drag trying to gather as much speed as possible for the 14-mile Alleghany climb just ahead. The Fort Spring Tunnel was bored in 1946-47 to eliminate a long, speed-restricting curve around the mountain as the railway followed the Greenbrier River.
Gene Huddleston, C&O Historical Society Collection

A Geep-powered coal drag exits Big Bend Tunnel at Talcott, West Virginia in September of 1959. Big Bend is the site of the John Henry legend. When the tunnel was being bored in 1870-73, John Henry was supposed to have beaten an early version of the steam drill in a contest. A ballad, which now has appeared in hundreds of versions, began, and John Henry has become an enduring symbol of man against machine in the Industrial Revolution. He has become, fact or myth, the black Paul Bunyan.
C&O Railway, C&O Historical Society Collection

Four Geeps have a westbound empty coal train rolling fast past the neat station at Quinnimont, West Virginia, deep in the mist-shrouded New River gorge. Three F7's can be seen in the distance picking up extra loads brought here from the Piney Creek Branch serving the Raleigh/Fayette coal fields. The line in the foreground goes up Laurel Creek to serve more mines.
C&O Railway, C&O Historical Society Collection

High-wave F's growl hard as they bring coal east around the sharp curve in the New River near Blue Hole, West Virginia in June of 1957. The New River gorge was once a beehive of industrial activity with coal mining, coke production, and a teeming population, but by the 1940's most of this was disappearing as the coal deposits near the river played out. Since then the area has returned to wilderness and is now partially preserved by a new National Park.
Gene Huddleston, C&O Historical Society Collection

The neat brick station at Cotton Hill replaced an earlier wooden structure in 1942, and though there are no other buildings within some distance in any direction, it did a big business serving people who came down from Fayetteville, a few miles to the south and the seat of Fayette County. Here five Geeps bring coal east for Tidewater — about 550 miles to go! The ancient New River, second oldest river on earth, with its rocky shoals, is to the right.
C&O Railway, C&O Historical Society Collection

At Gauley, West Virginia, the Gauley and New Rivers join to form the Kanawha, which flows west to the Ohio. Here three E's bring Train No. 6, *The Fast Flying Virginian*, east at Kanawha Falls, where the broad river takes a sudden plunge. This September, 1959 photo shows the new practice of using three units for combined trains between Ashland and Charlottesville, begun a year or so before.
C&O Railway, C&O Historical Society Collection

Handley, West Virginia, was the division point separating the New River Subdivision running from Hinton and the Kanawha Subdivision running to Russell, Kentucky. This 1954 photo shows three Geeps about to take a train west and a K-4 class 2-8-4 "Kanawha" type passing with a loaded train for the east in the days when steam and diesel worked side-by-side in this region. Handley was recently eliminated as a yard in the ever-changing face of American railroading.
C&O Railway, C&O Historical Society Collection

RSD-5's Nos. 5591 and 5575 make a mine run with empties on the Cabin Creek Branch near Leewood, West Virginia in April of 1954. The Alco's replaced H-4 and H-6 Mallets that had held sway in this service for many years as well as small Consolidations.
Gene Huddleston, C&O Historical Society Collection

The F's also traveled the branch lines, though certainly not as frequently as switchers and road switchers, since branch line work usually meant switching, which the cab units simply weren't intended for. Here two A-units bring loads off Cabin Creek at Ronda, West Virginia in 1954.
C&O Railway, C&O Historical Society Collection

RSD-7 No. 6805 has just arrived with a train at St. Albans, West Virginia as H-6 class 2-6-6-2 No. 1490, also an Alco product from 1920, sits on the ready track. This photo is typical of the transition days between steam and diesel on the C&O in April of 1956. The last steam runs would be made in October of that year.
Gene Huddleston, C&O Historical Society Collection

The Coal River Branch, out of St. Albans, stretched deep into the coal-mining districts of southern West Virginia and even today generates about a fourth of the C&O's coal traffic. Here, in June of 1959, three brand-new F7's take empties up the branch out of St. Albans as the fireman waves with both hands to the photographer!
Gene Huddleston, C&O Historical Society Collection

These empties, with an odd (for C&O practice) A-B set of F's, the A-unit in the new paint scheme and the B-unit in the old, are rolling along the Kanawha Subdivision mainline, having originated in the huge yard at Russell, Kentucky. They are bound for St. Albans to go up the Coal River Branch. This photo was made at Blue Sulphur Springs, West Virginia in June of 1957.
Gene Huddleston, C&O Historical Society Collection

This rare photo shows an E8 set in the first, freight-style, paint scheme with an eastbound passenger train (probably No. 6, *The FFV*) coming out of a westerly sun in 1953 near Milton, West Virginia.
C&O Railway, C&O Historical Society Collection

Alco RSD-12's replaced H-4 and H-6 2-6-6-2 Mallets one-for-one in the Logan, West Virginia coal fields, where they were used for mine shifters and to carry trains up the branch to the main at Barboursville and on to Russell. The C&O crews called these units "Dragon Ladies" because of their unusual appearance and distinctive growl. Here the 6701's engineer gets his orders at FD Cabin at Logan, West Virginia while enroute to the mines in August of 1956. The water tank in the background is still in active use for the steamers still operating in this same service.
Gene Huddleston, C&O Historical Society Collection

Huntington, West Virginia, was the western terminal of the C&O from 1873 until the Cincinnati Division mainline was built down the Kentucky side of the Ohio River and across the river into Cincinnati in 1888. It became the C&O's mechanical headquarters and one of the road's most important cities. Created from scratch by the C&O, it became West Virginia's largest city. Here a set of FP7's takes a manifest freight west through the yards. The large Colonial-style passenger station built in 1918 is visible in the right background.
C&O Railway, C&O Historical Society Collection

This scene has a certain Wagnerian appeal as Train No. 2, *The George Washington*, poses for the C&O's photographer in the Huntington yard while steam locomotives in the background throw up a pall of smoke and steam. This picture was taken on a cold night in December of 1952, just a few months after the E8's took over passenger service.
C&O Railway, C&O Historical Society Collection

Huntington's 16th Street yard is the setting for this scene featuring Baldwin AS-616 road switcher No. 5529 in 1955. C&O sampled Baldwin products but stuck with EMD and a dash of Alco in its first-generation diesels.
C&O Railway, C&O Historical Society Collection

The C&O bought two Alco RS-1 switchers in 1953, both equipped with steam generators for passenger train shifting. They were stationed at Huntington where they worked until transfer to the B&O in 1966. Here No. 5114 works on freight chores in front of the Huntington passenger station during a break in the passenger operations.
C&O Railway, C&O Historical Society Collection

FP7 No. 800 was painted solid black with a zebra-striped nose about 1960 as an experiment in improving visibility to cut down on grade crossing accidents. This photo shows the unit just out of the Huntington paint shop and ready for the road. The experiment was inconclusive and only a single GP9 was painted similarly at the same time as the F.
C&O Railway, C&O Historical Society Collection

Huntington Shops, mecca of steam in earlier times, by 1955 had been converted almost totally to diesel work. Here a variety of first-generation units are undergoing repairs in the main erection bay. In the foreground is an Alco RSD-7, followed by a Baldwin AS-616, an EMD BL2, an Alco RSD-5, an EMD GP7, and finally a GP9. What a variety! Huntington remained the C&O's main shop in the diesel era and took over most of the B&O's work in the 1970's. In 1987 it was designated as the main locomotive repair facility for the entire CSX Rail Transportation system, encompassing the old C&O, B&O, Western Maryland, Clinchfield, L&N, SAL, ACL, and several smaller roads.
C&O Railway, C&O Historical Society Collection

Rarest of the rare photos is this view showing BL2 No. 1839 with a Geep on a freight train at Catlettsburg, Kentucky. During their last few years some of the BL2's came to Ashland, Kentucky for use on the Kentucky sections of *The George Washington* and *The FFV* between Ashland and Louisville. This particular unit must have been out on a freight as a break-in after shopping.
C&O Railway, C&O Historical Society Collection

Ashland's passenger station was the largest on the system supporting strictly C&O trains, as trains from the Cincinnati, Hocking, Big Sandy, Kanawha, and Lexington Subdivisions converged here. *The FFV* and *The George Washington* were consolidated at Charlottesville and then broken up at Ashland with sections going to Cincinnati and to Louisville. Likewise the consolidated *Sportsman* from Charlottesville was broken and sent to Cincinnati and Detroit. The station had three umbrella sheds, a large coach yard to service cars, a commissary for the diners which were largely centered here, and a huge station building housing the facilities as well as divisional offices. Here a pair of E's leads an eastbound train, probably No. 6, *The FFV*.
C&O Railway, C&O Historical Society Collection

GP9 No. 5999 has a short train of empty hoppers coming out of the huge Armco steel plant at Ashland, Kentucky. Armco was and is one of the C&O's biggest customers, consuming huge quantities of iron ore, coal, and other supplies. This 1964 photos shows C&O's typical local switching practice with two cabooses, one with the locomotive and one at the train's end.
C&O Railway, C&O Historical Society Collection

An Alco RSD-7 six-motor unit brings a heavy coal train into Russell singlehandedly. These units were put to work on the Logan coal district, replacing 2-6-6-2 Mallets one-for-one. A few months before this October, 1956 photo would have seen a 1948-vintage H-6 2-6-6-2 pulling this same train from the marshalling yard at Peach Creek, West Virginia to Russell for classification and re-shipment.
C&O Railway, C&O Historical Society Collection

During the 1955-56 resurgence of steam, GP9 No. 5997, new from EMD in December of 1955, rubs couplers with big and little steam in the cold winter air at Russell engine terminal. *C&O Railway, C&O Historical Society Collection*

F-units were very common at Russell since they were regular power on through manifests and on the trains to Toledo as well as having other mainline duties. Here a set of three in the "high wave" paint moves an empty coal train through the huge yard.
C&O Railway, C&O Historical Society Collection

Alco RSD-5's were used at Russell as hump engines. Here a pair ride over the new Fitzpatrick yard at Russell. Built in 1958 for manifest freight classification and known as "Sputnik" because of its sophisticated electronic-operated systems, it seems primitive now 30 years later.
C&O Railway, C&O Historical Society Collection

5042
CHESAPEAKE & OHIO
5042
CHESAPEAKE & OHIO 219

ERIE
CHESAPEAKE & OHIO

September of 1955 finds an Alco S-2 switcher pulling an earlier Alco product, 0-8-0 No. 219, out of storage at Russell to be returned to service in the great locomotive shortage that occasioned the revival of steam.
Gene Huddleston, C&O Historical Society Collection

A C&O TR3 set is shown here leaving Russell as road engines on manifest freight No. 92 in September of 1949 during the great coal strike, when some of the yard diesels were pressed into road service to conserve coal. The TR3's were bought for the Russell hump and spent most of their lives there in the high-tractive-effort, low-speed hump service for which they were built. An 0-8-0 works in the background. The TR3's were essentially an NW2 locomotive with two semi-permanently-coupled boosters without cabs and C&O was to be EMD's only customer for the unique locomotives.
Gene Huddleston, C&O Historical Society Collection

"The End"

Russell was the C&O's largest and busiest engine terminal and its largest and busiest yard, so it stands to reason that it had a large shop for running repairs. Here sets of F-units are in the Russell shop for repairs and servicing in 1954.
C&O Railway, C&O Historical Society Collection

Vitally important to C&O coal business was and remains the Big Sandy Branch, running south from Ashland and tapping the rich eastern Kentucky coalfields. Here two Geeps bring a heavy train of coal down the branch towards Russell about 1960.
C&O Railway, C&O Historical Society Collection

The Big Sandy wasn't just important for coal. It served as an important conduit for perishable and other fast freight connecting with the Clinchfield Railroad at Elkhorn City, Kentucky, for the South. Here F7 No. 7040 takes Clinchfield No. 95 at Elkhorn City for its trip down the Big Sandy to the C&O main in September of 1952.
B.F. Cutler, C&O Historical Society Collection

The C&O's entire fleet of EMD TR4 cow-and-calf units is shown here at Dawkins, Kentucky with a train of coal bound for Paintsville on the Big Sandy main stem in June of 1958. These units were purchased specifically for the Dawkins Branch to handle trains that had required as many as four 2-6-6-2 Mallets to get over one particularly steep grade. They were used exclusively on the Big Sandy until transfer to the B&O in the late 1960's.
Gene Huddleston, courtesy H. H. Harwood, Jr.

FP7 No. 8002 as a single unit rolls Train 39 up the Big Sandy Subdivision in 1958 with four head-end cars and two coaches. The Big Sandy sustained passenger services until fairly late for branch lines—1963—the locomotive-hauled trains being replaced by RDC's about 1960.
C&O Railway, C&O Historical Society Collection

This 1952 view shows a pair of brand-new E8's with the Louisville section of *The George Washington*(Train No. 21) arriving at Anchorage, Kentucky where it moved from C&O tracks to Louisville & Nashville trackage rights. *The FFV* and "The George" both had Louisville sections highly patronized until Amtrak eliminated them in its new system in 1971. The C&O's Lexington line, once the haven of these passenger trains and several hot manifest freights, was recently abandoned and taken up!
Boyce Martin, C&O Historical Society Collection

An F7 A-B-A set led by the 7068 brings an empty coal train across the Ohio River on the giant Limeville bridge bound for Russell. The C&O Northern, later the Northern Subdivision, was built in two stages: in 1914-1917 and in 1926. It linked the Cincinnati Division mainline with the C&O-controlled Hocking Valley lines to get coal efficiently to Columbus and on to Toledo over the HV. To get across the Ohio, the Limeville bridge (also known as the Sciotoville bridge from the town on the Ohio side) was built to last forever and assume any amount of traffic. It was, for many years, the longest continuous truss span in the world and is still the strongest bridge ever built, with the highest combined live and dead load capacity of any bridge.
C&O Railway, C&O Historical Society Collection

September of 1958 finds three F-units taking a mixed freight and coal train north (west by the timetable) over the massive Limeville Bridge towards Columbus and Toledo. The size of this great C&O engineering feat can be appreciated in this angle taken from the cliffs on the Ohio side looking down on the north approach viaduct, the main spans of 775 feet each over the navigation channels of the river, and the Kentucky hills in the distance.
Gene Huddleston, C&O Historical Society Collection

The engineer running a set of F's picks up orders at CH Cabin, Parsons Yard, in Columbus, Ohio in November of 1952. The second group of F7's was used, in part, to dieselize the old Hocking Valley lines in Ohio and this set of engines has undoubtedly just bumped a 2-6-6-6 Allegheny type from the coal-hauling job on the Northern Subdivision and the Hocking Division mainline north of Columbus.
W.P. Ellis, C&O Historical Society Collection

Night at Parsons Yard engine terminal just south of Columbus finds FP7 No. 8004 and GP9 No. 6024 awaiting assignments on January 29, 1959.
C&O Railway, C&O Historical Society Collection

Three brand-new F's bring 85 loads out of Columbus on the steep grade at Powell, Ohio on July 20, 1953. The straight, flat lay of the mainline north of Columbus belies its subtle but important grades that affected operating patterns perhaps more in the steam era than after the diesels arrived.
Dick Action, Sr., David Orozzi Collection

If this wasn't their first road trip, it was certainly amongst their first as this set of really shining F's led by the 7071 beings a coal train north past Marion's Union Station, crossing the Erie mainline on May 4, 1952.
Dick Action, Sr., David Orozzi Collection

Alco RSD-5 No. 5582 sits on the Walbridge Yard turntable at Toledo in July of 1956 as a set of FP7's in freight service, headed by the 8009, passes in the background.
C&O Railway, C&O Historical Society Collection

A single GP9 powers a short freight train across the New York Central diamonds at Toledo, Ohio about 1959. The C&O took more of its coal westward to Toledo for dumping into boats on the Great Lakes than it took to the sea at Newport News. Manifest freight on this line was, however, less important.
C&O Railway, C&O Historical Society Collection

Walbridge Yard at Toledo on a night in 1953 finds a trio of first-order, high-wave-painted F7's getting ready to fuel up at the new facility in the shadow of the coal dock from steam days. The nose of another F-unit is seen to the right in an evocative scene of nighttime railroading in the early diesel era.
C&O Railway, C&O Historical Society Collection

Stevens yard was built at Silver Grove, Kentucky to serve the C&O needs at Cincinnati since the road couldn't get any suitable terminal within the city itself. This yard and one on the Chicago Division, north of the city, served the C&O along with the remnants of one at Covington, Kentucky, just across from Cincinnati. An Alco S-2 switcher works the yard here in January of 1950, while the smoke from steamers drifts up in the background. Stevens, Covington, and Cheviot yards are all now closed and C&O facilities have been consolidated with the B&O and L&N on B&O land in Cincinnati.
C&O Railway, C&O Historical Society Collection

The 7068 leads a trio of F7's out of Cincinnati in April of 1956 on the westward run to Chicago. The engineer picks up his orders as the train begins the climb up the steep grades and the high trestles of the Mill Creek valley. Like most urban areas, trackage and terminals in the Covington-Cincinnati area, including the bridge over the Ohio River, were owned by a number of terminal companies in which the C&O had varying interests. Once clear of the terminal area, the trains would be back on C&O's own trackage.
Herbert H. Harwood, J&D Studios Collection

On leaving Cincinnati, the C&O's Chicago Division mainline climbed out of the valley of Mill Creek on steep grades and over seemingly endless spindly bridges to attain the yard at Cheviot, a few miles out of the city. From Cheviot the trains would traverse the hill-and-dale line across Indiana, missing any really sizable cities, and linking the C&O to the great hub at Chicago. Here F-units move up the Cheviot Hill line out of Cincinnati on one of the high bridges in April of 1955. This line has now been abandoned and taken up.
C&O Railway, C&O Historical Society Collection

Baldwin AS-616 No. 5533 switches Cheviot Yard in Western Cincinnati in April of 1955. The coal dock and sand tower still stand in the background and a new yard office in the foreground.
C&O Railway, C&O Historical Society Collection

A set of simplified-paint-scheme F's powers a boxcar freight in the Wabash River valley near Peru, Indiana, carrying merchandise between the C&O's eastern and southern markets and the Great West via Chicago. The Chicago Division line had no branches and little local traffic. Most of its trains were through fast freights bridging the state of Indiana and giving the C&O a longer haul than when it had to exchange with the Big Four or other lines in Cincinnati before acquiring its own Chicago line in 1910. Gene Huddleston captured this scene in June of 1958.
Gene Huddleston, C&O Historical Society Collection

An F7B gets fuel at the Peru, Indiana engine terminal in 1957. In the steam days the C&O and Nickel Plate shared terminal facilities at Peru. Both roads were under the same ownership during and after the Van Sweringen days up until 1947 when the C&O sold its NKP stock. It looks like the 7510 has also gotten a washing down.
C&O Railway, C&O Historical Society Collection

The Chicago line was populated principally with K-2, K-3, and K-3a class 2-8-2 Mikados in the steam era because of the light bridge loadings and some tight clearances, so it was never host to any of C&O's big power. It was also a line-haul railroad with few switching districts and was ideal for the introduction of the diesel F7 road locomotives in 1951. The F's continued to populate the line, hauling its fast freight, until their transfer to the B&O. This April 12, 1950 view shows No. 7011 and its mates leaving Muncie, Indiana.
Arthur B. Johnson

This view of F's leaving C&O's Rockwell Street Yard in Chicago was used widely in the railway's fast freight publicity. The train is starting out for the Chicago Division and Cincinnati, where it will be reworked at Stevens Yard in Kentucky and forwarded over the old mainline to the coast.
C&O Railway, C&O Historical Society Collection

Rockwell Street Yard is again seen in this photo of GP7 No. 5859 taking a short freight out on the main. Rockwell Street was C&O's connection with the other great trunk lines, east and west, serving Chicago.
C&O Railway, C&O Historical Society Collection

C&O and B&O passenger trains shared Chicago's Grand Central Station, which the B&O largely owned. The C&O E7 seen here has *The Pere Marquette* on its drawbar waiting to leave for Grand Rapids, while the B&O unit is probably ready to take a mainline train east, perhaps *The Capitol*. The photo was made by C&O public relations photographers on May 15, 1961 for use in C&O/B&O merger publicity work. *C&O Railway, C&O Historical Society Collection*

The C&O's wholly-owned subsidiary, the Pere Marquette Railway, got the first diesels in the C&O family when it purchased SW1's from EMD in 1939. More switchers arrived in 1942 and 1943. This EMD NW2 arrived in February of 1943 and survived several renumberings and transfer to the C&O in 1976. Here it appears in the mid-1940's in its original black paint with gold steam locomotive lettering.
C&O Railway, C&O Historical Society Collection

Pere Marquette NW2 No. 59, EMD class of 1946, waits for assignment at the PM diesel house in Chicago in July of 1947. The more colorful paint was adopted in 1946 and was retained by some of the switchers even after they were relettered C&O. The basic body is blue, the thick stripes are yellow, and the accent stripes around them are red.
C&O Railway, C&O Historical Society Collection

Detroit's Union Station was a massive red brick strucuture that looked much like a medieval cathedral with its Romanesque architecture and large clock tower. Called Fort Street Union Station, it served trains of the PM, C&O (*The Sportsman* from Newport News), the Pennsylvania, Ann Arbor, and others. Of course in later days the PM colors disappeared in favor of the C&O. The C&O eventually assumed complete ownership of the terminal railway that owned the station and demolished it after the end of passenger service. In better days—1959—E8 No. 4012 has *The Sportsman* ready to leave for Columbus, Ashland, Charleston, Charlottesville, Richmond, Newport News, and Washington. Detroit's skyline looms in the background.
H.H. Harwood, Jr.

This is an unusual photo showing a PM/C&O E7 painted gold and sporting special logos commemorating the production of 50 million General Motors automobiles. It powered a special train of GM officials and is seen here in April of 1955 at Plymouth, Michigan. After the one trip the locomotive was repainted back into its C&O colors!
C&O Railway, C&O Historical Society Collection

E8 No. 4001 handles Pere Marquette District passenger train No. 25 at Walhalla, Michigan in September of 1958. As the C&O's passenger fleet began to decline, it was able to shift the E8 fleet to help the E7's with the PM District trains. In the mid-1960's, the E7's all went to the B&O and the E8's supplanted them entirely in Michigan.
W.P. Ellis, C&O Historical Society Collection

The Thornapple River bridge near Grand Rapids was a favorite location for both railway photographers and railfans. Here a pair of GP7's leads a fast freight over the river's frigid water in the winter of 1955. Note that these units don't have the dynamic brake blisters that are evident in the photos of Geeps on the Chesapeake District. Dynamic braking is an ingenious idea which converts the traction motors into generators. The train's momentum on a downgrade is consumed in generating electricity, which is shunted through resistors in the brake blisters and dissipated as heat. The Geeps bought for the PM lines didn't need the dynamic brakes, since there were no heavy grades to handle.
C&O Railway, C&O Historical Society Collection

This wonderful posed photo at the Wyoming Yard roundhouse in Grand Rapids shows GP7 No. 5766, E7 No.102, E7 No. 107, and NW2 No. 5211 in 1954. By this time the C&O was beginning to publicize their dieselization rather than being shy about it as they were at first. Since the PM District had been all-diesel since mid-1951, it was an ideal place to photograph units in their natural habitat. Note the differences between the 102 and the 107 in the placement and size of the number boards. The 102 has received the C&O tricolor paint, but the 107 is still in the PM livery, though it sports the C&O herald.

C&O Railway, C&O Historical Society Collection

Purely Pere Marquette, E7 No. 104 is ready to take the *Pere Marquette* out of Grand Rapids Union Station's trainshed in 1949, while a similar E7 in the same paint but with the C&O "doughnut" herald on its nose waits on an adjacent track. Both still have their coupler cowls, but they are different styles.
C&O Railway, C&O Historical Society Collection

Brand new at the roundhouse at Wyoming Yard in Grand Rapids, Pere Marquette E7 No. 102 is ready for its first assignment in August of 1946, that of carrying a demonstration train of *Pere Marquette* cars to the principal cities the train would serve as a promotional ploy. The rumps of mighty 2-8-4 Berkshires are seen in the stalls.
C&O Railway, C&O Historical Society Collection

This 1959 view of Wyoming Yard diesel shop with many of its residents lounging in the open was a common scene from the beginning of dieselization until Grand Rapids was demoted in status after the CSX merger and its shops closed. Evident on this day are Geeps and a BL2.
C&O Railway, C&O Historical Society Collection

BL2 No. 1844 gets a rebuilt engine at the Wyoming diesel shops in 1954. Major repairs were done here for all the locomotives assigned to the Northern Region until the 1970's, when much of the work was transferred to Huntington. This is a wonderful view of EMD's famed 567 engine that powered the BL2's. These locomotives have become somewhat of a darling among diesel fans because of their rarity and homely looks.
C&O Railway, C&O Historical Society Collection

BL2 No. 82 was delivered in June of 1948 with a number assigned by PM but lettered for C&O since the merger had intervened. It is seen here in Detroit about 1950 still wearing its original paint scheme with the pale yellow — hardly discernible in a black-and-white photo — extending all the way up its "chain guard" area. Later versions brought the blue down to a straight line above the road name.
C&O Railway, C&O Historical Society Collection

C&O E7 No. 96, lettered both C&O and PM, has a six-car train on its drawbar in this publicity photo taken in 1948. The Budd-built stainless-steel cars were originally for *The Chessie*, Robert Young's dream train for the Cincinnati-Washington daylight coach trade. When passenger business eroded, the C&O canceled this train before it ran more than a single demonstration trip and reassigned the cars to the PM District. They were used to inaugurate a new set of *Pere Marquette's* between Grand Rapids and Chicago, hoping that they would repeat the success that similar trains had had between Grand Rapids and Detroit. One of *The Chessie's*'s dome-observation cars is on the rear in this consist as well. When the C&O's large Pullman-Standard passenger car order arrived in 1950, the Budd cars were sold. One strange thing about this photo is the steam locomotive and passenger car just behind the train. It was probably a business car on the rear of the train that the engine detached for the photographer's pictures.
C&O Railway, C&O Historical Society Collection

GP7's Nos. 5718 and 5776 leave Ludington, Michigan with a freight in 1957. Ludington was the Pere Marquette's great port, where freight cars were placed on huge modern car ferries and taken across Lake Michigan to three ports on the Wisconsin side where they were transferred to other railroads. This avoided the terminal delays and costs in Chicago and was a great business until recent years. This train is made up of cars that have undoubtedly arrived from Milwaukee, Kewaunee, and Manitowoc in Wisconsin and are bound perhaps for Buffalo and points east using the old PM as a bridge line.
C&O Railway, C&O Historical Society Collection

C&O GP7's Nos. 5720 through 5738 were built by General Motors Diesel, EMD's Canadian plant at London, Ontario and were used exclusively on the C&O's Canadian Division that connected Detroit and Port Huron in Michigan with St. Thomas, Ontario, where trackage rights sent the C&O trains over the New York Central's Canadian lines to Buffalo. Here the 5736 brings a merchandise freight over the brand-new bridge at Wallaceburg, Ontario in 1959.
C&O Railway, C&O Historical Society Collection

At Port Huron the C&O operated car floats that carried its cars over the St. Clair River to Sarnia, Ontario. This February, 1952 view is very rare in that an E7 and a passenger train are at Sarnia on the Canadian side. Passenger service had evaporated from the Canadian Division long before dieselization. This occasion was a special train for Dow Chemical Company executives and had come in from Detroit by using the tunnels to Windsor, Ontario and then had come up the C&O to Sarnia. Dow has a huge chemical plant here that gives the C&O much business.
C.A. Butcher

This high bridge at St. Thomas was always an ideal spot for dramatic photos and the C&O photographer used it to good advantage to capture two GMD GP7's and their train in 1957.
C&O Railway, C&O Historical Society Collection

On the far east end of the C&O's Canadian service its trains reentered the United States and terminated at Buffalo, New York. Here two Geeps lead a fast freight over the fabulous steel arch bridge at Niagra Falls about 1955.
C&O Railway, C&O Historical Society Collection